¡Sé las reglas!

¡COMPARTO!

Por Bray Jacobson

Please visit our website, www.garethstevens.com. For a free color catalog of all our high-quality books, call toll free 1-800-542-2595 or fax 1-877-542-2596.

Library of Congress Cataloging-in-Publication Data

Names: Jacobson, Bray, author.
Title: ¡Comparto! / Bray Jacobson.
Description: Buffalo, New York : Gareth Stevens Publishing, [2024] |
    Series: ¡Sé las reglas! | Includes index.
Identifiers: LCCN 2022051552 (print) | LCCN 2022051553 (ebook) | ISBN
    9781538290910 (library binding) | ISBN 9781538290903 (paperback) | ISBN
    9781538290927 (ebook)
Subjects: LCSH: Sharing–Juvenile literature. | Benevolence–Juvenile
    literature.
Classification: LCC BJ1533.G4 J348 2024 (print) | LCC BJ1533.G4 (ebook) |
    DDC 177/.7–dc23/eng/20221230
LC record available at https://lccn.loc.gov/2022051552
LC ebook record available at https://lccn.loc.gov/2022051553

Published in 2024 by
Gareth Stevens Publishing
2544 Clinton Street
Buffalo, NY 14224

Copyright © 2024 Gareth Stevens Publishing

Designer: Claire Wrazin
Editor: Kristen Nelson
Translator: Michelle Richau

Photo credits: cover EvgeniiAnd/Shutterstock.com; p. 5 Twinsterphoto/Shutterstock.com;
pp. 7, 24 (crayons) Daniel Jedzura/Shutterstock.com; p. 9 Alexander Safonov/
Shutterstock.com; p. 11 GagliardiPhotography/Shutterstock.com; pp. 13, 24 (snack) littlenySTOCK/
Shutterstock.com; p. 15 Iryna Inshyna/Shutterstock.com; p. 17 Tomsickova Tatyana/
Shutterstock.com; pp. 19, 24 (apple) Hananeko_Studio/Shutterstock.com; p. 21 Billion Photos/
Shutterstock.com; p. 23 Natalia Lebedinskaia/Shutterstock.com.

All rights reserved. No part of this book may be reproduced in any form without
permission in writing from the publisher, except by a reviewer.

Printed in the United States of America

CPSIA compliance information: Batch #CSGS24: For further information contact Gareth Stevens, at 1-800-542-2595.

Find us on

Contenido

Compartir en escuela 4

Compartir los tentempiés 12

Compartir en familia . . . 16

Palabras clave 24

Índice 24

¡Comparto!
Es una regla en la
escuela.

Dennis dibuja un
dibujo.
Él tiene una caja de
ceras.

Patti le pide usar
las ceras.
Ella dice por favor.
¡Dennis comparte!

Leighton tiene el balón grande.
Ella se lo pasa a Don.
Ellos comparten.

Queda un tentempié.
Drew lo quiere.
Holden lo quiere.

La maestra lo divide en
dos partes.
Los chicos comparten
el tentempié.

Comparto en casa.
Dejo que mi hermano
juega con mi carrito.
¡Él me lo devuelve!

La manzana de Andrea
sabe buena.
Ella le da a su mamá
un trozo.

¡Ellas comparten la fruta!

¿Cómo puedes compartir?

Palabras clave

manzana　　　　cera　　　　tentempié

Índice

casa, 16　　　　escuela, 4

ceras, 6, 8　　　tentempié, 12, 14